MW01121674

CHANTEZ ENCORE
FOLKSONGS OF FRENCH SOUTH LOUISIANA

Selections, Settings, and Annotations

BY JEANNE & ROBERT C. GILMORE

PELICAN PUBLISHING COMPANY
GRETNA 1991

Library of Congress Cataloging in Publication Data
Main entry under title:

Chantez encore.

Reprint. Originally published: Acadiana Music, 1979
Bibliography: p.
Includes index.
1. Folk music—Louisiana. 2. Folk-songs, French—
Louisiana. I. Gilmore, Jeanne. II. Gilmore, Robert C.
M1629.7L8C5   1984   84-4983
ISBN 0-88289-425-0 (pbk.)

Manufactured in the United States of America
Published by Pelican Publishing Company, Inc.
1101 Monroe Street, Gretna, Louisiana 70053

TABLE OF CONTENTS

(CONTINUED ON NEXT PAGE)

TABLE OF CONTENTS
(CONTINUED)

Dedication

This book is dedicated to Irène Thérèse Whitfield Holmes, author of <u>Louisiana</u> <u>French</u> <u>Folk</u> <u>Songs</u>, the definitive work in the field.

Acknowledgements

People, here and abroad, who have given us songs and other kinds of help, are accorded acknowledgement and thanks in the body of the book, always in proximity with a song or group of songs.

Additionally, however, there are several professionals whose superior contributions to the production of this book merit, we feel, special recognition. To the following, such is herewith tendered:

To Charles H. Reynolds, for expert musical/pianistic editing; to Terry C. Girouard, whose beautiful art work graced our first book and who, happily, does an encore for this one; to Kenneth Duhon, for the distinctive music manuscript; and to Mrs. Rita B. Patout for the excellent typing.

CHANTEZ ENCORE

Preface

The "Encore" in the above title provides the clue, for this book is indeed an invitation to sing again the songs of French Louisiana. In the early seventies we had the rare good fortune of putting together a modest little work titled Chantez, La Louisiane! which to our delight became - and remains - a best seller of its kind. The present work, Chantez Encore, actually began with the debut of the first book, because we collected far more songs - great tunes - than we could use in our initial effort. And secondly, the first book brought forth literally hundreds of comments, such as "Fine, but it's too short; do another". And, of course, "Why didn't you include this and that".

Well, the "this and thats" have been piling up for several years now. And so have many, many experiences - with folklorists, school people, children, and most especially, with a general public which grew far in excess of our fondest dreams.

Too, our research for Chantez Encore has gone far beyond that done for the earlier book. This, as the bibliography will show, has included just about everything written on the subject in this country, plus an extended visit to French Canada, and most recently (Summer 1976), three months in the French provinces of Brittany, Normandy and Poitou. Because we were so impressed with the latter experience, we have broken with our prior "Louisiana only" policy and included five songs from these provinces.

Yet another experience, this one prompted by CODOFIL* resulted in the inclusion of a group of "Christmas Songs in French".

Lastly, we have included a section titled, "Learning French by Singing French", with the hope that it will be of interest and help to teachers. This section sets forth a rationale and procedure for teaching French folk songs in a bilingual program. For the past seven years we have done demonstrations for music, French and classroom teachers, plus long-term projects with children. The essence of this experience is presented in this section. Also, wherever appropriate, "Teaching Tips" have been included in the "Notes about the Song".

We herewith proffer our deepest appreciation to the many who embraced our first book, and in doing so, ordained Chantez Encore as a "command performance". For us, the two have constituted a long, rich and rewarding experience, one that, happily, shows no signs of diminishing.

JLG
RCG

*Council for the Development of French in Louisiana

"This is Mrs. Jeanne Marie Landaiche Veron of Donaldsonville (La.)
speaking", the voice on the phone said, "and I'd like to have a couple
of copies of your Chantez, La Louisiane! Where can I get them?"
After being told, she went on to ask, "By the way, did you ever hear
La Mère Acadie?" When I said no, she replied, "Well, I'm not sur-
prised. My mother used to sing it, and even though it's a great song,
I've never found anybody who has heard or seen it anywhere. Would you
like to hear it?" I said yes and she ripped it off, "tout entier",
and over long distance yet! We sent her two complimentary copies
of our Chantez, La Louisiane! in the next mail.

As you will see, Mrs. Veron was right - La Mère Acadie is a great song.
And it is unknown and unique. We have sung it a number of times over
Louisiana, in France and in French Canada and have found no one who
knows it.

It is unique in two respects. The swinging 6/8 (in two), while quite
common in the folk songs of France and Canada, is rare indeed in the
indigenous songs of South Louisiana. Further, we know of no other
Louisiana French folk song that deals with French Canada, despite the
famous (or infamous) expulsion of the Acadians from Nova Scotia (then
Acadia) in 1755. So, a fair assumption would seem to be that La Mère
Acadie is of Acadian origin, or possibly, a rare Louisiana offspring
inspired by that ill-fated exodus from Grand Pré. The words are
Standard French.

Teaching tip: Note that in the melody, the rhythm and especially the
words, the first two lines (Too-roo-too-too) are quite similar. The
3rd and 4th lines are melodically different but the rhythm therein
stays much the same. You will note there is a D.C. at the bottom,
which, of course, means go back to the beginning and sing the first
two lines again, stopping at the "Fine". "Roll the 'r' when you sing
Too-roo-too-too" Mrs. Veron told us. The translation which follows
is hers.

    Too-roo-too-too (sound the fanfare) for Mother Acadia:
    She is dead, (bis) she exists no more.
    She willed for her heritage, some bread, some butter,
    some cheese, and some salt (in her wooden shoes)
    for salting her beans.

La Mère Acadie

A sprightly two-to-the-bar

Too-roo-too-too pour la Mère A - ca-die: elle est morte; elle est morte.

♩. = 120

Too-roo-too-too pour la Mère A-ca-die: elle est morte, elle ex - iste non plus! Elle

Fine

(2nd time: a bit slower and broader to end)

a lai-ssé pour hé - ri-tage du pain, du beurre et du fro-mage,

Et du sel, dans ses sa - bots, pour sa - ler ses ha - ri-cots.

D.C.

Poco rit.

1

Notes about Il a Tout Dit   (France-French origin)

In putting together a collection such as this, certainly, the people
one meets constitute a most rewarding part of the endeavor. Always,
they are as interesting as the songs they so willingly give you. Mrs.
Lillia LaBauve of Abbeville (La.) who gave us Il a Tout Dit in the
summer of 1970 is indeed such a person. She is not only a delightful
and talented lady, but a pioneer and an authority in the field of
Louisiana French folk music, a fact to which we can readily attest,
having found her name many times during our research.

"I'm fairly sure it's France-French", says Mrs. LaBauve of Il a Tout Dit
Indeed it is, for this Summer (1976) in Normandy we found it to be
well-known. And no wonder it has lasted. The contours and sequences
in the melody are most appealing, the harmonies natural and satisfying,
the rhythm is that of a flowing, gentle waltz and the lyrics tell an
engaging tale. The words, of course, are Standard French.

Teaching tips: Repetition - in the melody, rhythm figures and words -
makes the song very easy to learn and remember. Note that the melody
of the verses (lines 1 & 2) and the melody of the refrain (lines 3 & 4)
is almost identically the same. And it's easy to harmonize. Observe
that the right hand part of the piano accompaniment carries the melody
and a simple harmony part. It goes well with autoharp or guitar chords.
The key of G would be easier for guitar. An English approximation
would go about thus:

        When I was young, I knew the handsomest boy in the village
        But he became fickle and I liked him no longer.
Refrain: He told all, (repeats)
        He told everything I told him.

        But he changed, and he asked me to marry him.
        We were married in the village church.
Refrain: He no longer told all, (repeats)
        He no longer told everything I told him.

        And here is our family, five boys and four girls.
        They were baptized in the village church.
Refrain: He has not said, (repeats)
        He has not said that this is the end.

Il A Tout Dit

Gentle waltz

Verses

1. J'ai con - nu dans mon jeune â - ge le plus beau gar-con du vil - la - ge,
2. Mais il est de - ve - nu sa - ge m'a de - man - dé en ma - ria - ge,
3. Et voi - ci no - tre fa - mil - le cinq gar - çons et qua-tre fil - les;

♩ = about 88

1. Mais il est de - ve - nu vo - la - ge, et de - puis je ne l'ai - me plus.
2. Dans l'é - gli - se du vil - la - ge, nous nous som - mes ma - ri - és.
3. Dans l'é - gli - se du vil - la - ge, nous les a - vons bap - ti - sés.

Refrain

Il a tout dit, tout dit, tout dit, il a tout dit, tout dit, tout dit, tout dit,
Il n'a plus dit, plus dit, plus dit, il n'a plus dit, plus dit, plus dit, plus dit,
Il n'a pas dit, pas dit, pas dit, il n'a pas dit, pas dit, pas dit, pas dit,

Il a tout dit, tout dit, tout dit, Il a tout dit c'que j'lui a - vais dit.
Il n'a plus dit, plus dit, plus dit, il n'a plus dit c'que j'lui a - vais dit.
Il n'a pas dit, pas dit, pas dit, il n'a pas dit que c'e -- tait fi - ni.

3

This beautiful Creole lament (or "complainte" as the French call it) is in our Chantez, La Louisiane!, but in a shortened, simplified version, since we had a primary focus on classroom usage. From the outset, however, it was felt that the abbreviated setting was an injustice to the song. The one presented here, hopefully, corrects this.

Both Cable and Monroe (see bibliography) suggest a West Indian origin for Zizi and refer to it as "One of the best Creole love songs" (Cable) and also as "... universally known and sung on Louisiana plantations... Cable tells us too that the famed Gottschalk, a Creole himself, used the melody in one of his celebrated (if somewhat flamboyant) piano arrangements, concert performances of which brought him international acclaim around the mid 19th century.

The singer is Zizi's lover and his song is one of sympathetic lamentation. Zizi suffers bitter jealousy because one "Calalou" (a derisive name for a quadroon) has received and is showing off finery that she would like to have. The Creole-dialect words translate about as follow

> Poor little Miss Zizi,
> Her heart is sore.
> Calalou wears madras,
> She wears lace petticoats.
> Poor little Miss Zizi,
> Her heart is sore.

About the two codas for Zizi: As you doubtless know, "coda" means "ending piece" or, a final section of a song. At the end of the 1st page, you will find, "To coda, next page." On the top of the next page you will find a simple eight bar coda, designated just "coda". Below this simple coda you will find a 2nd coda, designated "Optional coda", which has a not-so-simple, harp-like piano accompaniment written under the melody. You have a choice - the top or simple coda, or the more elaborate optional coda. (Arranger's note: I must confess that I "lifted" this optional coda. We found it in an article, Creole Slave Songs, by George Washington Cable, published in Century Magazine, dated April 1886. I liked it and could not resist.)

5

Momzelle Zizi

Coda

Pauv' pi -ti Mom -zelle Zi -zi, pauv' pi - ti Mom -zelle Zi -zi,

A tempo

Li gai -gnain bo -bo, bo -bo, dans so pi - ti tchoeur. *Fine*

Optional coda

Pauv' pi -ti Mom - zelle Zi -zi, pauv' pi - ti Mom -

A tempo

zelle Zi -zi, li gai -gnain bo - bo, bo - bo,

dans so pi - ti tchoeur. *Fine*

Except in mode, Zélime and Zizi have much in common. (The first is major, the second is minor.) Both are Creole laments, sung by the male about a loved one. Too, both are outcries prompted by a situation over which those involved had no control.

Most important, however, is that Zélime (like Zizi) is of incomparable beauty, largely attributable to an exceptionally fine contour in the melodic line. And this gives the melody a most expressive, natural-sounding rise and fall, both as to pitch levels and degrees of tension and relaxation. It has been said of Beethoven that his melodies (or themes) were so well put together, the next note always seemed inevitable. It is so with Zélime. The melody can stand completely alone, even without the very moving words.

We are much indebted to Mrs. Lise Wehrmann Wells of New Orleans for granting us permission to use the beautiful setting of Zélime made by her late father, the musicologist, Henri Wehrmann. It appears in his excellent book, "Creole Songs of the Deep South", published in 1946 by the Philip Werlein Company of New Orleans, and is still available.

Teaching tip: Notice that the 1st, 2nd and 4th lines are melodically identical, with the 3rd being different. This means that when the 1st line is learned, one knows three-quarters of the melody. There is little repetition in the words. But, the Creole French sings beautifully. (All of those difficult French sounds are eliminated!)

The translation which follows is that of Professor Wehrmann.

> Zélime has gone from the plantation, I have lost you,
> Dearest one.
> Both my eyes cry like a fountain, since I lost you,
> Dearest one.
> At night, in my cabin, I am dreaming dear, of you.
> In the daytime, in the cane field, I am thinking
> Dear of you.

Zélime

Zé - lime, to quit-té la plai - ne, di-pi qu'mo pli' mi-ré toué; zié a

moin sem - blé fon - tai - - ne, di-pi qu'mo pli' gar-dé toué. La

nuit dan' mo ca-ba - - ne, dan' dra' mi mo son-gé toué, le jou'

A little faster   Broaden   Dim.   A tempo

quan' mo cou-pé can - ne, c'est en - cor' toué qu'mo son - - gé.

9

Notes about Pas Loin de Chez Moi   (Cajun French)

Whitfield (see bibliography) believes that this typical Cajun song probably came from the Parish of Lafayette since one Toto Simoneaux did have a dance hall just out of Carencro (La.) some years ago. She goes on to say, "It is rumored that he had the longest beard in Lafayette Parish, and that he parted it in two and tied it at the back of his neck".

As implied, it has the genuine flavor of the Cajun waltz. The lilt, the swing, the drive on beat one - all are typical of the genre. But it is not average; it is well above. It is a great tune that bespeaks the essence of its cultural roots in the most engaging manner. This belief is buttressed by the fact that the composer Virgil Thomson used it prominently in his score for the great documentary film, "Louisiana Story".

If the words seem to make little sense - well - who said they had to? For that matter, Toto Simoneaux's beard doesn't make much sense. (Maybe it would today.) An English approximation would go about thus:

Not far from my home I met Philomène Domingue. She told me there would be a dance at Toto Simoneaux's. No use for you to holler, no use for you to jump; my heart is yours, and your heart is mine.

We are indebted to our good friend, Professor Charles H. Reynolds, pianist/composer at the University of Southwestern Louisiana (Lafayette), for this stomping piano accompaniment.

Pas Loin de chez Moi

Bright, swinging

Pas loin de chez moi, j'ai ren - con - tré Phi-lo-mène Do - mingue. Elle m'a

(One to the bar)

♩. = 60

dit qu'il y a-vait bal chez Toto Si - mo - neaux. C'est pas la

peine t'en ti cries, c'est pas la peine t'en ti sautes; Mon

coeur se - rait a toi, et ton coeur se - rait a moi.

11

Notes about Mon Amour Est Barré (Cajun French)

When Virgil Thomson wrote the score for the prize-winning documentary film, "Louisiana Story', he first obtained a copy of <u>Louisiana French Folk Songs</u> by Irène Thérèse Whitfield, the definitive work in the field. <u>Mon Amour</u> was one of the many Cajun tunes that he used from this authentic source, and certainly one of the most moving. After completing the film score Thomson wrote to Miss Whitfield (now Mrs. Holmes), saying, "Thank you for your beautiful tunes". Since he made prominent use of the song as a sequence piece in the film score, he was doubtless as impressed as we are today with its poignant beauty. Actually, in flavor, it is quite "uncajun".

Translation

My love is locked in the "armoire" (wardrobe),
And the key is hidden in my heart.
Last night I had you in my arms,
But I found it was only a dream.

Mon Amour Est Barré

Mon a - mour est bar - ré dans l'ar-moire, et la clef est ca - chée dans mon

coeur. Hier au soir j'a-vais toi dans mes bras, mais j'ai

trou - vé que c'é - tait un rêve.

Gently, legato

♩ = 72

Notes about the Mardi Gras song (Cajun French)

In two distinct but related respects, the Mardi Gras song is unique in its category, namely that of the Louisiana Cajun folk tune. First, it is in the minor mode, a rarity for the genre. Secondly, while the words chronicle the main event of a very gay, hilarious celebration, its quite distinctive melody projects an aura of sadness. This incongruity, however, seems prophetic rather than paradoxical when one recalls that the penitential season of Lent begins with Ash Wednesday, the next day. That is, this song, in an eerie, mystical way, gives expression to an almost frantic frivolity while serving as a precursor of the period of penance which culminates with the tragedy of Good Friday. The hypothesis here is that the song's distinctive character is thus accounted for.

While there are several Louisiana Mardi Gras songs we associate this one with Mamou, having heard it there a number of times. However, back in 1971, Mr. Shirley Bergeron of Church Point gave us a copy of the words upon which this version is, in the main, based. Quite recently we got into the arduous task of taking down the musical notation, doing so principally by playing, over and over, all of the recordings of it we could find. To our knowledge, there is no other musically notated version, and we've a good idea why. It's the toughest tune we've ever tackled. The difficulty encountered was not with the words, but with the melody, this being attributable mainly to the fact that folk singers care not for the niceties of consistent rhythmic/melodic phrasing.

But making this "written down" version was a labor of love, for a prime purpose was to make more widely available a truly great Louisiana French folk song. Learn it, and go to the Mardi Gras. You'll "pass much pleasure." And too, you'll find this song expresses the essence of an unforgettable celebration. About the words. Since there are many versions and verses, we chose three stanzas that seemed best in catching the mood and principal elements of the Mardi Gras Ride of Mamou. By the way, the "Capitaine", the only unmasked rider, carries a flag and leads the ride.

Translation

Verse 1. Captain, Captain, wave your flag; let's get on the road.
　　　　　 Captain, Captain, wave your flag; let's go to the other neighbor's.
　　　　　 The Mardi Gras (riders) get together once a year to ask for charity.
　　　　　 They go once a year, all around the hub.

Chorus: The Mardi Gras (riders) come from everywhere, yes, my good comrade.
　　　　　 The Mardi Gras   "   come from everywhere, all around the hub.

Verse 2. They come from everywhere, but mainly from Grand Mamou.
　　　　　 They come from everywhere, all around the hub.
　　　　　 Will you welcome this band of Mardi Gras?
　　　　　 Will you welcome this band of big drunks?

Chorus: The Mardi Gras (riders) ask the master and the mistress if they may come in.
　　　　　 The Mardi Gras   "   ask very politely if they may come in.

Verse 3. Give us a little fat hen to make a rich gumbo.
　　　　　 Give us a little rice, all around the hub.
　　　　　 The Mardi Gras (riders) thank you for your good will.
　　　　　 The Mardi Gras   "   thank you for your good will.

Coda: Captain, Captain, wave your flag; let's get on the road.
　　　　 Captain, Captain, wave your flag; let's go to the other neighbor's.

14

Mardi Gras

Verse 1

Ca-pi-taine, Ca-pi-taine, voy-age ton flag, allons se mettre dessus le ch'min.

Marche, driving

♩ = 108

Ca-pi-taine, Ca-pitaine, voy-age ton flag, al-lons al-ler chez l'autre voi-sin.

Les Mar - di Gras s'ras-semblent pour de - man - der la cha - ri - té.

Ça passe une fois par an, tout à l'en- tour du moy - en.

Les Mar-di Gras de-viennent de tout par-tout, oui, mon cher bon ca-ma - rade.

Loud, excited

Les Mar -di Gras de-viennent de tout par-tout, mais tout à l'en -tour du moy-en.

Cont. loud, excited

15

GRAND MAMOU

Mardi Gras

Ils viennent de tout par-tout, mais prin-ci-pale-ment d'Grand Ma - mou.

Verse 2   g   Eb   F   F7   d

Ils viennent de tout par - tout, tout à l'en - tour du moy - en.

g   Eb   c minor   F7   d   g

Vou - lez - vous rec'- voir mais cette bande de Mar - di Gras.

g   Eb   F   F7   d

Vou - lez - vous rec'- voir mais cette bande de grands sou - lards.

g   Eb   c minor   F7   d   g

Les Mar -di Gras de-mandent mais la ren-trée au maître et la maî - tresse.

Loud, excited   g   Bb   d c minor g   F7   d

Les Mar - di Gras de-mandent mais la ren-trée a-vec tous les po - li-tesses.

(As above)   g   Bb   d c minor F7   d   g

16

Mardi Gras

Don - nez-nous autres une 'tite poule grasse pour faire un gom - bo gras.

Verse 3   g   Eb   F   F7   d

Don - nez-nous autres un peu du riz tout à l'en - tour mon a - mi.

g   Eb   c minor   F7   d   g

Les Mar - di Gras vous r'mer - cient bien pour votre bonne vo - lon - té.

g   Eb   F   F7   d

Les Mar - di Gras vous r'mer - cient bien pour votre bonne vo-lon - té.

g   Eb   c minor   F7   d   g

Ca-pi-taine, Ca-pi-taine, voy-age ton flag, al-lons se mettre des-sus le ch'min.

Loud,
excited   g   g   Bb   d   c minor g   F7   d

Ca-pi-taine, Ca-pi-taine, voy-age ton flag, al-lons al-ler chez l'autre voi-sin.

Fine

(As above) g   g   Bb   d   c minor F7   d
g

17

Notes about C'est Pas La Bague   (Cajun French)

This Cajun love song, a lament, is an arrangement of another gem
from the incomparable Whitfield work. (See bibliography) A fairly
literal translation would be about thus: It isn't the ring (I gave
her) that I hate to lose; it's the coat my girl friend gave me.
Whitfield explains that when a young maiden gave a "coat" to her lover,
("a donné un capot") it signified, in Cajun, that he was to leave her
house and never return.

C'est Pas la Bague

C'est pas la bague que j'ai re - gret - tée,
C'est le ca - pot que ma belle m'a don - né.

(Sadly, but
not too slowly)

♩ = 100

Notes about A Paris   (France-French origin)

Even without the words, A Paris has a melodic flavor that is un-
mistakably France-French. And speaking of the words, we've taken
some liberties with the second and third verses ("A Gueydan" and
"A Pont Breaux") by inserting the names of two well-known towns in
the Acadiana area of South Louisiana.

Translation: To Paris, to Paris, on a little grey horse
               To Gueydan, to Gueydan, on a little white horse
               To Breaux Bridge, to Breaux Bridge, on a little
               galloping horse.

Notes about Il Est Midi   (France-French origin)

This charming folk verse was given to us by Dr. Adèle Cornay St. Martin,
Professor of French at the University of Southwestern Louisiana. It
is well known in France and in French Louisiana. The melody is of the
authors' contrivance. It was written in Dinan, France (Brittany) this
past Summer (1976), under the inspiration of Madame Dequé who helped
us greatly in our research. She, like us, thought that Il Est Midi
should have a French sounding musical setting. We wrote this one and
sent it back to her.

                        Translation

          It is noon. Who said so? The little mouse.
          Where is she? In the chapel.
          What is she doing? Making lace.
          For whom? For the ladies of Paris.

A Paris

Easy, gentle

♩ = about 88

A Pa-ris, à Pa-ris, sur un pe-tit che-val gris. A Guey-dan, à Guey-dan, sur un pe-tit che-val blanc. A Pont Breaux, à Pont Breaux, sur un p'tit ch'val à gal-op.

* a minor may be used on autoharp

Il Est Midi

Quietly

♩. = about 58 Tempo ad lib

Il est mi-di. Qui l'a dit? La p'tite sou-ris. Où est elle? Dans la cha-pelle. Que fait elle? De la dentelle. Pour qui? Pour les dames de Pa-ris.

21

In 1970 we trained a "French Choir" (Les Jeunes Acadiens) at the Hamilton Elementary School in Lafayette. (La.) They sang only Louisiana French folk songs. Upon the occasion of their singing for the French Consul from New Orleans, we needed a short, snappy closing number. So we took this well-known tongue twister, contrived a fitting ditty, and voila! It worked. (Confidentially, it "passed" for a Louisiana French folk tune.)

Teaching tip: Repetition makes this little song very easy to learn. The 1st and 2nd lines are identical. The 3rd and 4th lines (though different from the first two) are also identical. The words, of course, are quite repetitive. And they translate: Your tea? Has it removed your cough?

22

Ton Thé

Lively

♩ = 126

Ton thé a-t-il ôté ta toux, ton thé, ta toux?

Ton thé a-t-il ôté ta toux; ton thé, ta toux, ton thé?

Loudly

Ton thé, ta toux? Ton thé, ta toux, ton thé?

Softly

Ton thé, ta toux? Ton thé, ta toux, ton thé?

23

Notes about Mo L'aimé Toi, Chère   (Creole French)

While this well-known little chant for children is in the Creole
dialect, the melody is markedly Cajun. Perhaps this is an example
of the "fusion of French and African traditions (which) left a per-
manent imprint in the form of satirical songs in French Louisiana"
of which Brandon writes. (See bibliography) Incidentally, this was
one of the many songs suggested when we were doing our first book.
So, here it is at last, Miss Odette Coussan of Carencro, La.

Translation

I love you dear, with all my heart, dear.
My woolen dress, my "Grecian band";
It is all for you dear,
It is all for you.

Mo L'aimé Toi, Chère

Bouncy

Mo l'ai - mé toi chère, 'vec tout mon coeur, chère, mo

robe de laine, mo "Gre - cian band", c'est tout pou' toi chère;

C'est tout pou' toi chère.

Notes about Mon Bon Vieux Mari   (Cajun French)

We are indebted to Mr. Donald Hebert, St. Landry Parish Supervisor of Music (La.), for introducing us to "My Good Ol' Man", certainly one of the most unique, melodically charming and hilariously amusing Cajun songs in French Louisiana. It is unique because (as noted before) the 6/8 (in 2) meter is rare in Cajun tunes. And too, the infectious melody which swings the comic tale along so well is not French at all; melody and words are of British origin, via Appalachia. (For more see Brandon and Oster in Bibliography.)

The song is in the form of a dialogue between an admiring wife, who sings the verses, and her "Bon Vieux Mari" (the best drinker in the land) who replies with spoken, growled-out answers.

Translation

Wife (singing)

1. Where are you going, my good old husband,
   Where are you going, the one they call love?
   Where are you going, my good old husband,
   The best drinker in the country?

Husband (speaking)   I'm going to the cafe.

2. What will you do there, my good old husband,
   What will you do there, the one they call love?
   What will you do there, my good old husband,
   The best drinker in the country?

   I'm going to get drunk.

3. When will you return, my good old husband,
   When will you return, the one they call love?
   When will you return, my good old husband,
   The best drinker in the country?

   Tomorrow or another day.

4. What shall I cook for you, my good old husband,
   What shall I cook for you, the one they call love?
   What shall I cook for you, my good old husband,
   The best drinker in the country?

   A gallon of couche-couche and a dozen eggs.

5. That could well kill you, my good old husband,
   That could well kill you, the one they call love?
   That could well kill you, my good old husband,
   The best drinker in the country?

   That doesn't matter; I have to die anyway.

6. Where do you want me to bury you, my good old husband,
   Where do you want me to bury you, the one they call love?
   Where do you want me to bury you, my good old husband,
   The best drinker in the country?

   Bury me in the chimney corner, and from time to time,
   Pass me a hot potato.

Mon Bon Vieux Mari

1. Et où c' que t'es par - ti, mon bon vieux ma - ri?
2. Et quoi t'es par - ti faire, mon bon vieux ma - ri?
3. Et quand c' que tu re - viens, mon bon vieux ma - ri?
4. Et quoi tu veux j'te cuise, mon bon vieux ma - ri?
5. Ça pour - rait bien te tuer, mon bon vieux ma - ri?
6. Et où tu veux j't'en-terre, mon bon vieux ma - ri?

♪. = 138 Jaunty, swinging two-to-a-bar

1. Et où c' que t'es par - ti, ce qu'on ap - pelle l'a - mour?
2. Et quoi t'es par - ti faire, ce qu'on ap - pelle l'a - mour?
3. Et quand c' que tu re - viens, ce qu'on ap - pelle l'a - mour?
4. Et quoi tu veux j'te cuise, ce qu'on ap - pelle l'a - mour?
5. Ça pour - rait bien te tuer, ce qu'on ap - pelle l'a - mour?
6. Et où tu veux j't'en- terre, ce qu'on ap - pelle l'a - mour?

1. Et où c' que t'es par - ti, mon bon vieux ma - ri?
2. Et quoi t'es par - ti faire, mon bon vieux ma - ri?
3. Et quand c' que tu re - viens, mon bon vieux ma - ri?
4. Et quoi tu veux j'te cuise, mon bon vieux ma - ri?
5. Ça pour - rait bien te tuer, mon bon vieux ma - ri?
6. Et où tu veux j't'en- terre, mon bon vieux ma - ri?

1-6. Le meil - leur bu - veur du pa - ys.

Réponses.
1. Parti au café.
2. Parti me souler.
3. Demain ou un autre jour.
4. Un gallon de couche-couche et une douzaine d'oeufs.
5. Ça fait pas rien, j'ai pour mourir quand même.
6. Enterre-moi dans le coin de la cheminée, et temps en temps, passe-moi une patate chaude.

Notes about Elle Descend de la Montagne (American/French)

This highly comical version of "Comin' Round the Mountain", en français, was given to us by Mr. Owen Demourelle, Director of the Evangeline Parish (La.) Bilingual Program. Owen learned it from French student teachers in Angers, France.

Verse one states that "She'll come down the mountain on horseback," and in the 2nd, "She'll kiss her Grandpa as she comes down." In verse 3 the singer states, "I'd like to be her Grandpa", but in the 4th concludes, "I'd prefer to be twenty years old and have all of my teeth."

The teaching/learning merits are rather obvious. First, of course, is the familiarity of the American folk song. Next, the words are quite repetitive. Thirdly, the spirited melody kicks the words along, making the song real fun to sing. Note that the piano accompaniment, written separately from the melody, provides a syncopated, driving lift to the song.

28

Elle Descend de la Montagne

In a recently authored short treatise (1976, Three Louisiana French Musics), we advanced the theory that Louisiana Creole folk songs are unsurpassably unique, in that there is no other indigenous Black music known in this country that is even remotely like these Negro French folk songs. Broadly, they tend to be of two types: flowing laments and/or love songs, or, happy, highly rhythmic, witty/satirical, catchy tunes, of which Caroline is an example. However, despite its generic uniqueness, Caroline is no museum piece, but, as you will see, a most enjoyable song to learn and sing. Too, the words provide some excellent examples of the Creole dialect, and the singability thereof. The translation is that of Professor Henri Wehrmann, the New Orleans musicologist.

> One, two, three, Caroline, tell us what the trouble is. (repeats)
> Papa says no, mama says yes; 'tis she I love, 'tis she I'll have.
> We're out of funds to buy a home.
> 'Tis she I love, 'tis she I'll have.

Caroline

Notes about Ah! Mon Beau Château   (France-French
(The Anna Belle Hoffman Version)   origin)

"When I was a little girl we used to play this 'choosing game' as
we sang Ah! Mon Beau Château. Being very young we would become
embarrassed as there was a choosing of a boy or girl involved."
Thus spake Anna Belle Dupuis Hoffman Krewitz of Breaux Bridge (La.)
when she gave us this Louisiana version of a singing game which is
well-known in France, Canada and French Louisiana. Mrs. Krewitz,
who has been called "a one-person Chamber of Commerce for Breaux
Bridge" - and indeed, for Acadiana - justly enjoys a front row position
among the distinguished people associated with the renaissance
of the French language in South Louisiana. She is both a founding
spirit and an epitomization of this now well-known bilingual program.
Fitting recognition has come her way. She is a charter member and
past president of France Amérique de la Louisiane Acadienne, a reci-
pient of the Palmes Académiques Award from the French government and
holds an honorary doctorate from Loyola, New Orleans.

Now, to the song. Of all the versions encountered - in Louisiana,
Canada ('75) and this Summer ('76) in France - we like the Anna Belle
Hoffman/Louisiana version best, largely because it has the most
interesting melodic contour. Excellent instructions for the singing
may be found in Les Danses Rondes by Theriot and Blanchet. (See
bibliography) Since so much repetition is involved, note that an
optional piano accompaniment is provided. A translation follows.

1. Ah my beautiful castle, va t'en li le li le la.
    Ah my beautiful castle, "   "   " " " " "

2, Ours are finer, va t'en li le li le la.
    Ours are finer, "   "   " " " " "

3. Which stone will you carry off, va t'en li le li le la.
    Which stone will you carry off, "   "   " " " " "

4. I will take Madame Durand, va t'en li le li le la.
    I will take Madame Durand, "   "   " " " " "

5. What will you give, va t'en li le li le la.
    What will you give, "   "   " " " " "

6. I will give M'sieu Girard, va t'en li le li le la.
    I will give M'sieu Girard, "   "   " " " " "

7. She says she'll take him, va t'en li le li le la.
    She says she'll take him, "   "   " " " " "

8. She says she won't take him, va t'en li le li le la.
    She says she won't take him, "   "   " " " " "

Ah! Mon Beau Château

With spirit

♩ = 132

	D	D	D G	D

1. Ah! mon beau châ — teau, va t'en li le li le la.
2. Les nôtres sont plus beaux, va t'en li le li le la.
3. Quelle pierre enl' - v'rez — vous, va t'en li le li le la.
4. C'est Ma — dame Du — rand, va t'en li le li le la.
5. Qu'est c'que vous donn — 'rez, va t'en li le li le la.
6. J'donn-rai m'sieu Gi — rard, va t'en li le li le la.
7. Elle dit qu'elle en veut, va t'en li le li le la.
8. El — le n'en veut pas, va t'en li le li le la.

D	D	A7 ✱	D

1. Ah! mon beau châ — teau, va t'en li le li le la.
2. Les nôtres sont plus beaux, va t'en li le li le la.
3. Quelle pierre enl' - v'rez — vous, va t'en li le li le la.
4. C'est Ma — dame Du — rand, va t'en li le li le la.
5. Qu'est c'que vous donn' — rez, va t'en li le li le la.
6. J'donn-rai M'sieu Gi — rard, va t'en li le li le la.
7. Elle dit qu'elle en veut, va t'en li le li le la.
8. El — le n'en veut pas, va t'en li le li le la.

✱ Small notes optional.

Optional piano accompaniment

N.B. Key of C may be used to better fit autoharp.

33

Notes about La Délaissée   (France-French origin)

"As in the case of the song I just sang for you" (Ah! Mon Beau Château)
Mrs. Anna Belle Hoffman Krewitz told us, "I learned La Délaissée
as a child. But these verses I give you now, we got from different
people in the Breaux Bridge (La.) area when we were doing research
in preparation for the 1955 Acadian Bicentennial." (This, of course,
was in commemoration of the 1755 expulsion order handed down by the
English to the Acadians at Grand Pré.) "Miss May Pellerin and I
went all around in my Model A collecting these verses", she continued.
"From place to place the verses varied, but the tune was always the
same. I remember, too, that Miss June Broussard and Miss Maria
Pellerin, both of Breaux Bridge, were chief contributors." Hence,
for her, quite naturally, the song identifies with the Breaux Bridge
area. However, word-of-mouth research indicates a France-French origin.

Notes given by Mrs. Krewitz describe La Délaissée as a "plaintive love
song, full of tenderness and pathos. It tells of a well-known character suffering pangs of unrequited love after an amorous adventure."
Thus spake the incomparable Anna Belle! A translation follows:

1. I am the jilted one, who cries night and day,
   The one who jilted me was my first love.
   "I thought you loved me, I loved you with all my heart.
   I see I was mistaken, and I must forget you."

2. "I was barely sixteen, lovely as a flower,
   Then you came and embittered my heart.
   Your charm, your caresses, your deceitful kisses,
   Your false promises - my tears fall on and on."

3. I see him every day, by my rival's side,
   Who, between tender kisses, speaks to him of love.
   In the same grave, death unites the lovers.
   The lovely girl is dead, as well as her deceitful lover.

4. Death is cruel indeed, a heartfelt blow.
   The lovely girl is dead, as well as her deceitful lover.
   In the same grave, death unites the lovers.
   The lovely girl is dead, as well as her deceitful lover.

La Délaissée

Plaintively.

1. Je suis la dé - lais - sée   qui pleu-re nuit et jour.
2. J'a-vais seize ans à pei - ne   bel-le comme u - ne fleur.
3. Je le vois cha - que jour   au-près de ma ri - vale,
4. La mort est bien cru-el - le   de nous frap-per au coeur.

♩. = 54

1. Ce - lui qui m'a lais - sée   é - tait d'mes pre-mières a - mours.
2. Il a fal-lu que tu vien - nes em - poi - son-ner mon coeur.
3. Qui lui par-lait d'a - mour   en - tre ses doux bai - sers.
4. Elle est bien morte, la bel - le, et son a - mant trom - peur.

1. Moi qui cro-yais que tu m'ai - mais,   moi qui t'ai-mais de tout mon coeur.
2. Tes charmes et tes ca - res - ses,   tes doux bai-sers trom - peurs,
3. Et dans la mê - me tom - be,   la mort doit nous u - nir.
4. Et dans la mê - me tom - be,   la mort doit nous u - nir.

1. Et main - t'nant je vois le con-traire,   Il fau - dra s'ou - bli - er.
2. Et tes faus-ses pro - mes - ses,   Me re-jettent dans les pleurs.
3. Elle est bien morte la bel - le,   Et son a - mant trom - peur.
4. Elle est bien morte la bel - le,   Et son a - mant trom - peur.

35

Notes about Devinez   (Cajun/English)

This delightful cumulative song is from the collection of Mrs. Catherine Brookshire Blanchet who is widely and most deservedly recognized as an authority on the Acadian folk music of South Louisiana. Her thesis, cited in the bibliography, is, we feel, one of the outstanding research endeavors in the field. Too, Mrs. Blanchet is not only a scholar and a native, but, most fortunately, an excellent, formally trained musician. The tasteful piano accompaniment here is hers.

Mrs. Blanchet feels that Devinez "is a product of the mixing of American (British) colonists and French émigrés. You might call it", she went on "a French translation of an English folk song." Hence it falls in the category of Mon Bon Vieux Mari (My Good Old Man) which is in this collection. The song was given to Mrs. Blanchet by a student, Purvis Hebert, during the course of her tenure as Supervisor of Music in Vermilion Parish. (La.) "There are many versions", she said, "and just about every person that I interviewed (in Vermilion) knew it."

Teaching tip: Because of the repetition, in melody and rhythm, this song can be learned quite readily. Note that the 1st and 2nd lines are identical. The 3rd and 4th lines (though different from the first two) are also identical. Too, it will be noted that there is considerable repetition in the words.

Translation

Guess what?

1. Guess what is in my father's field?
   Guess what is in my father's field?
   A little tree, a little tree,
   A little tree for Aunt Dolie.
   A little tree, a little tree,
   A little tree for Aunt Dolie.

2. Guess what is in the little tree?
   Guess what is in the little tree?
   A little nest, a little nest,
   A little nest for Aunt Dolie.
   A little nest, a little nest,
   A little nest for Aunt Dolie.

3. Guess what is in the little nest?
   Guess what is in the little nest?
   Little eggs, little eggs,
   Little eggs for Aunt Dolie.
   Little eggs, little eggs,
   Little eggs for Aunt Dolie.

4. Guess what is in the little eggs?
   Guess what is in the little eggs?
   Little blackbirds, little blackbirds,
   Little blackbirds for Aunt Dolie.
   Little blackbirds, little blackbirds,
   Little blackbirds for Aunt Dolie.

Devinez

Lively. ♩ = 112

F · F · F · F

De — vi — nez ce qu'il y a de — dans le clos d'mon père.
De — vi — nez ce qu'il y a de — dans le pe — tit arbre..
De — vi — nez ce qu'il y a de — dans le pe — tit nid.
De — vi — nez ce qu'il y a de — dans les pe — tits oeufs..

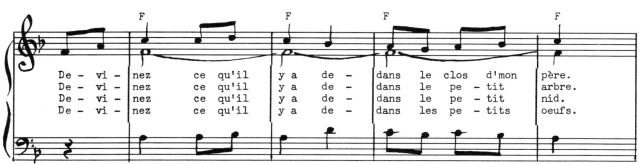

F · F · F · F

De — vi — nez ce qu'il y a de — dans le clos d'mon père.
De — vi — nez ce qu'il y a de — dans le pe — tit arbre.
De — vi — nez ce qu'il y a de — dans le pe — tit nid.
De — vi — nez ce qu'il y a de — dans les pe — tits oeufs.

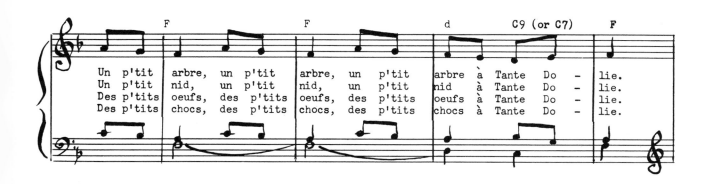

F · F · d · C9 (or C7) · F

Un p'tit arbre, un p'tit arbre, un p'tit arbre à Tante Do — lie.
Un p'tit nid, un p'tit nid, un p'tit nid à Tante Do — lie.
Des p'tits oeufs, des p'tits oeufs, des p'tits oeufs à Tante Do — lie.
Des p'tits chocs, des p'tits chocs, des p'tits chocs à Tante Do — lie.

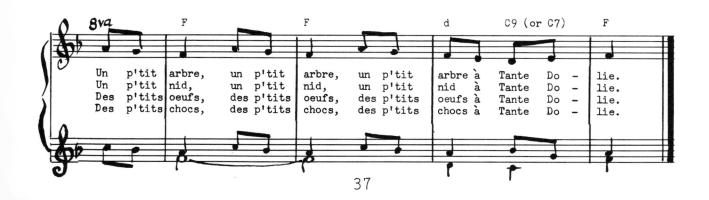

8va · F · F · d · C9 (or C7) · F

Un p'tit arbre, un p'tit arbre, un p'tit arbre à Tante Do — lie.
Un p'tit nid, un p'tit nid, un p'tit nid à Tante Do — lie.
Des p'tits oeufs, des p'tits oeufs, des p'tits oeufs à Tante Do — lie.
Des p'tits chocs, des p'tits chocs, des p'tits chocs à Tante Do — lie.

37

Like Devinez, Un, Deux, Trois is also from the collection of Catherine
Brookshire Blanchet. Mrs. Blanchet says she got it from the thesis of
Gaston Adam (see bibliography) and was given permission by him to
use it. She believes it to be quite old and doubtless of France-
French origin. Certainly it is the "classic type", especially with
regard to songs for children. A translation follows:

        1, 2, 3, we will go to the wood,
        4, 5, 6, I have cherries in my basket;
        7, 8, 9, my brand new basket,
        10, 11, 12, my bright (all) red basket.

Un, Deux, Trois

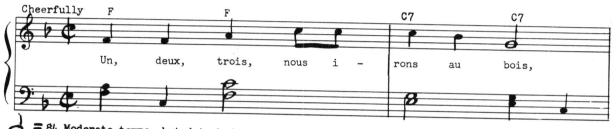

Cheerfully

Un, deux, trois, nous i - rons au bois,

$\stackrel{\circ}{} = 84$ Moderate tempo, but detached.

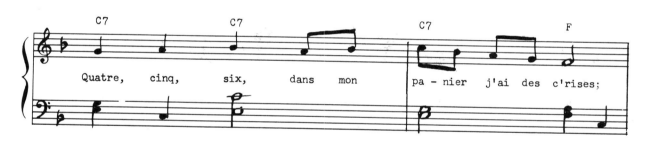

Quatre, cinq, six, dans mon pa - nier j'ai des c'rises;

Sept, huit, neuf, mon pa - nier tout neuf,

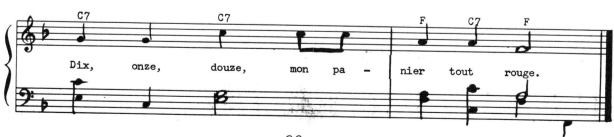

Dix, onze, douze, mon pa - nier tout rouge.

39

Notes about Bon Jour, Mes Amis   (France-French origin)

This attractive little teaching song is from <u>Chants</u> <u>et</u> <u>Jeux</u>, an excellent book of songs and games which was developed during the Summer of 1972 by the Lafayette Parish Bilingual Program, under the directorship of Dr. N. Ruth Bradley. We were pleased to contribute by transcribing the music from a number of tapes which had been made, for the most part, by young teachers from France. Hence, a fair assumption is that <u>Bonjour</u>, <u>Mes</u> <u>Amis</u> is a recent import. A translation is hardly needed, but in the interest of consistency - the first verse says, good day, my friends; the 2nd says goodbye, my friends; and the third, farewell, friends.

Teaching tip: Quite obviously, much repetition in the words makes the verses very easy to learn. Too, the bugle-like, happy tune will be easy to teach and remember. As a teaching song it is one of the best, especially because it's one that children will enjoy singing over and over.

Bonjour, Mes Amis

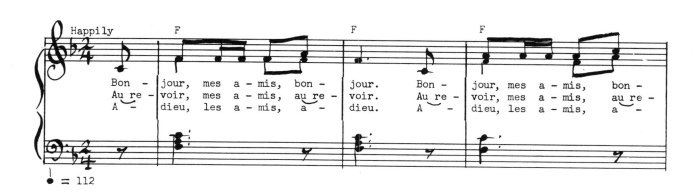

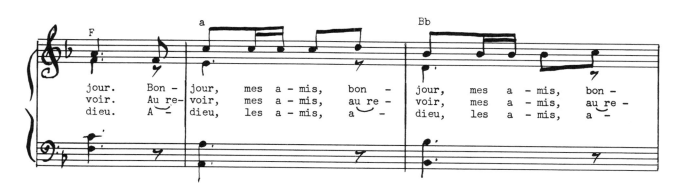

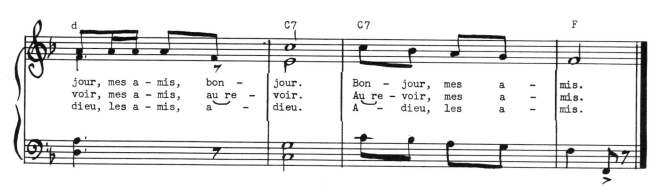

Happily   ♩ = 112

Bon - jour, mes a - mis, bon - jour. Bon - jour, mes a - mis, bon -
Au re - voir, mes a - mis, au re - voir. Au re - voir, mes a - mis, au re -
A - dieu, les a - mis, a - dieu. A - dieu, les a - mis, a -

jour. Bon - jour, mes a - mis, bon - jour, mes a - mis, bon -
voir. Au re - voir, mes a - mis, au re - voir, mes a - mis, au re -
dieu. A - dieu, les a - mis, a - dieu, les a - mis, a -

jour, mes a - mis, bon - jour. Bon - jour, mes a - mis.
voir, mes a - mis, au re - voir. Au re - voir, mes a - mis.
dieu, les a - mis, a - dieu. A - dieu, les a - mis.

Hommages À Nos Amis

About the Songs and the People
And Summer 1976 in France

The five songs which follow in successive pages were selected from literally hundreds obtained during three months of research in France this Summer. Actually, the primary purpose of the trip was not to collect songs, but to conduct interviews, mostly with folk music specialists, for a forthcoming book, tentatively titled Cajun Music - A Search for Its Roots. In the process we sang Cajun tunes for the interviewees and asked questions. In return we got not only answers but many, many songs.

And so, first by giving you five of their songs, we herewith dedicate a short portion of this book to those wonderful people over there who gave so freely of help and hospitality. Secondly, we wish to extend a special expression of appreciation to those whose names follow:

To Michel Lefort of Chatellerault, musician par excellence - thank you for "L'Alouette" - it's a real beauty - hope you like our arrangement of it; to M. Sylvain Arinal, the leading folklorist of Rouen - you gave us more songs, more time and more kindness than we had any right to expect; to M. André Pacher of Pamproux (near Poitiers) - thank you for the first real great interview of Summer '76 - do bring your gifts to Louisiana sometime; to M. et Mme Petiot of Dinan - you, your lovely town, les crêpes et le cidre et le beau dîner chez vous - all are cherished memories; to Mme Dequé, teacher and civic leader of Dinan and environs - merci, merci for that great Sunday (June 27), with the folk festival at Saint-Samson-sur-Rance, the tour of the countryside, the visits to castle Hunaudayne and the Vaumadeuc manor house - 'twas a glorious day; to M. et Mme Claude Masson, Journalist, Ouest-France at Lisieux - you must come to Louisiana for otherwise we can never reciprocate - how's your English coming?; to M. Roger Parment, Editor, Liberté Dimanche at Rouen - thank you for showing us your beautiful city and taking us inside so much of its history - thank you too for putting our pictures and some nice words about us in your paper; to M. Guy Barbedor of Rennes, Journalist of Ouest-France - we are most grateful to you for setting up our first interview of Summer '76; to Docteur et Mme Deviosse of Chatellerault - our warmest thanks for your hospitality and for introducing us to M. LeFort, Mlle Piault and M. et Mme Butruille; to Mayor Vertadier of Poitiers - we shall never forget the VIP treatment just because you knew our Mayor Kenny Bowen; to M. et Mme Théodore Taniou of Poitiers - our taste buds still twitter when we think of that enormous and delightful meal at Hotel Midi in St. Savin; to M. et Mme Georges Butruille of St. Sauveur - our thanks for the tour of the villages of Balzac and Rabelais with lunch (and folk singers) at Sache and the concluding visit to your home and farm; to Mayor René Regnault of Saint-Samson-sur-Rance - we recall with much pride the special welcome you gave us when we visited the folk festival in your town; and to L'Abbé Roger Abjean of St. Paul de Léon (near Roscoff) - thank you for the many books containing your arrangements of the songs of Bretagne and for your most gracious hospitality.

And there were many others who helped us in special, non-research related ways. To them all we are deeply grateful for a rich and rewarding Summer '76 in the provinces of Bretagne, Normandie and Poitou.

(Translations of the five "Summer '76 French Songs" follow on the next page.)

43

Translations of the Summer 1976 French Songs

L'Alouette

The lark and the blackbird want to get married
But there's no bread for the wedding breakfast.
Oh! my bird, how fine he is!

Along came Mister Crow, a piece of bread under his wing.
"Here is bread, but no meat will you have."
Oh! my bird, how fine he is!

Then came Mister Heron, carrying a ham under his wing.
"You'll have meat, but there'll be no wine."
Oh! my bird, how fine he is!

Here came a little mouse, with a barrel around her neck.
"Here is wine, but no music."
Oh! my bird, how fine he is!

Next came a fine, big rat, with a drum under his arm.
"Music you'll have, if you guarantee me protection from the cat."
Oh! my bird, how fine he is!

"I can protect you from the tomcat, but watch out for the tabby."
The tabby came down from the attic, and carried the drummer away.
Oh! my bird, how fine he is!

Qu'il Fait Chaud

How hot it is in the shed! I am wet to the bone.
I feel my flannel vest stick to my back.

Sur le Plancher

On the floor, a spider knits his socks,
In a jar, a snail spins his trousers,
I saw a honeybee strumming a guitar in the sky,
Rats, in confusion, rang the Angelus in the style of a fanfare.

Y a un Rat

There's a rat in the attic, I can hear the cat meow. (repeats)

D'où Viens-Tu, Bergère?

Where do you come from, little shepherdess?
I come from the stable where I saw the Infant Jesus
Lying on the fresh straw.

Is He beautiful, little shepherdess?
More beautiful than the moon and the sun.
Never on earth has His like been seen.

Anything else, little shepherdess?
Saint Joseph, His father, Saint John, His godfather,
And His good Mother who nurses Him.

Anything else, shepherdess?
Four little angels, down from Heaven,
Sing the praises of the Eternal Father.

L'Alouette

1. L'a-lou-ette an -vec* el* mar - lot* tous les deux veulent se ma - ri - er*
2. Il est ve -nu maî -tre cor - beau sous son aile ap -porte un chan-tiau*

♩. = 60 Flowing, pulsating, connected.

1. Tous les deux veulent se ma - ri - er* mais point d'pain pour leur dé -jeu-ner
2. Pour ♪ pain vous en au - rez ben* pour d'la viande vous en au - rez point

1. Oh! mon oi - seau qu'il est beau.
2. Oh! mon oi - seau qu'il est beau.

Slight rit., end of 2nd verse.

Verse 3 & 4
next page.

*
Glossaire

anvec	avec
ben	bien
chantiau	morceau de **pain**
el	le
marlot	merle

45

L'Alovette

3. Il est ve-nu maî-tre hé-ron sous son aile ap-porte un jam-bon
4. Il est ve-nu une p'tite sou-ris à son cou ap-porte un ba-ril

3. Pour d'la viande vous en au-rez ben pour du vin vous en au-rez point
4. Pour du vin vous en au-rez ben pour d'la mu-sique vous en au-rez point

* 3rd verse, stems up; 4th verse, stems down.

3. Oh! mon oi-seau qu'il est beau.
4. Oh! mon oi-seau qu'il est beau.

Verses 5 & 6
next page. Fermata short; and on end of 4th verse only.

46

L'Alovette

Faster ♩ = 100

5. Il est ve-nu un bon gros rat un tam - bour des - sous son bras
6. J'te ga-ran - ti-rons ben du chat mais d'la chatte tu te mé-fié - ras

5. Pour d'la mu-sique vous en au - rez ben si du chat m'ga - ran-tis - sez ben
6. La chatte a des - cend du gre -nier elle em-porte el tam - bou - ri -nier

* Stems down, 6th verse

Ending for 5th verse
Oh! mon oi - seau qu'il est beau.

Ending for 6th verse
Oh! mon oi - seau qu'il est beau.

Slowly

Qu'il Fait Chaud

Lively

$\bullet = 112$

Ah! quell' cha, ah! quell' cha, quell' cha - leur dans la ba - ra - que,

On est mou, on est mou, on est mouil-lé jus-qu'aux os,

On sent son, on sent son, on sent son gi - let d'fla - nel - le,

Col - ler à, col - ler à, col - ler à la peau du dos.

Sur le Plancher

Sprightly

Sur le plan-cher, une a-rai-gnée se tri-co-tait des bot-tes.

Dans un fla-con, un li-ma-çon en-fi-lait sa cu-lot-te.

J'ai vu dans le ciel, u-ne mouche à miel pin-cer d'la gui-ta-re.

Des rats tout con-fus son-ner d'l'An-ge-lus au son d'la fan-fa-re.

Y a un Rat

Briskly

Y a un rat   dans l'gre-nier,   j'en-tends le chat   qui   miau - le,

Y a un rat   dans l'gre-nier,   j'en-tends le chat miau -   ler,

♩ = 112

j'en- tends,   j'en - tends,   j'en - tends   le   chat qui   miau - le,

J'en- tends,   j'en- tends,   j'en- tends   le   chat miau -   ler.

50

D'où Viens-Tu, Bergère?

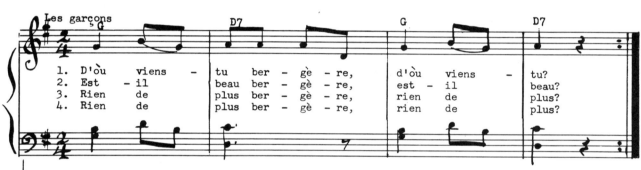

Les garçons

1. D'où viens - tu ber - gè - re, d'où viens - tu?
2. Est - il beau ber - gè - re, est - il beau?
3. Rien de plus ber - gè - re, rien de plus?
4. Rien de plus ber - gè - re, rien de plus?

♩ = 80 Gently, legato (avoid dragging)

Les filles

1. Je viens de la crê - che voir l'en - fant Je - sus.
2. Plus beau que la lu - ne et que le so - leil.
3. Saint Jo - seph son pè - re, Saint Jean son par - rain,
4. Qua - tre pe - tits an - ges des - cen - dus du ciel,

1. Sur la pail - le fraî - che il est é - ten - du.
2. Ja - mais sur la ter - re n'ai vu son pa - reil.
3. Et sa bon - ne mè - re qui lui donne le sein.
4. Chan - tent les lou - an - ges du père é - ter - nel.

Christmas Songs in French

Just before Christmas 1975, CODOFIL (Council for the Development of French in Louisiana) asked us to arrange some songs for a caroling program involving several hundred children. The program, managed by Dr. Georges Planel, came off very well and prompted the thought of including the songs in Chantez Encore. Dr. Planel gave us the French for the five songs whose titles follow. Since all, save the last, are well-known in English, a translation is given for Il Est Né only.

Vive le Vent (Jingle Bells) American
Nuit Etoilée (Silent Night) German
Mon Beau Sapin (O Christmas Tree) German
Les Anges dans Nos Campagnes (Angels We Have Heard on High)
    French
Il Est Né (He is Born) French

He is born, the Child Divine. Oboes, play; bagpipes, resound.
He is born, the Child Divine; let us praise His coming.
Here we are in the season of promise, foretold by all the prophets.
Here we are in the season of promise, invoked by our burning desire.

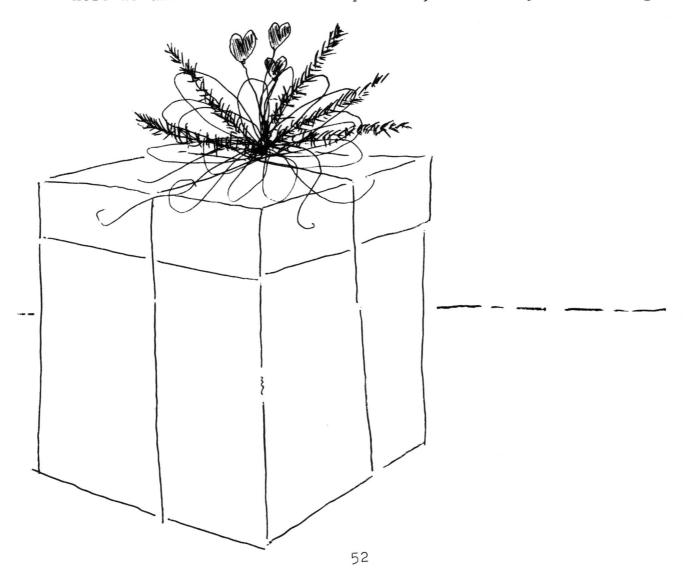

Vive le Vent

Vive le vent! Vive le vent! Vive le vent d'hi-ver!

Boule de neige! Jour de l'An! Et Bonne An - née, Grand' - mè - re!

Vive le vent! Vive le vent! Vive le vent d'hi - ver!

Boule de neige! Jour de l'An! Et Bonne An - née, Grand' -mère!

53

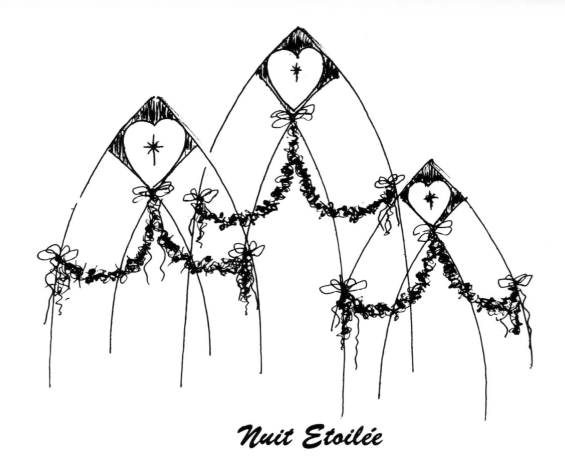

Nuit Étoilée

Bel - le nuit, dou - ce nuit, une é - toile nous con-duit

A l'é-ta - ble de l'En-fant qui vient de naî - tre main-te-nant

Sur l'hu-mi - de pail - le dans la nuit en plein vent.

Mon Beau Sapin

Mon beau sa-pin, roi des fo-rêts, que j'ai-me ta ver-du-re.
Toi que No-ël plan-ta chez nous au saint an-ni-ver-sai-re.

Quand, par l'hi-ver, bois et gué-rets sont de-pouil-lés de leurs at-traits
Jo-li sa-pin, comme ils sont doux et tes bon-bons et tes jou-joux

Mon beau sa-pin, roi des fo-rêts, tu gar-des ta pa-ru-re.
Toi que No-ël plan-ta chez nous par les mains de ta mè-re.

55

Les Anges dans Nos Campagnes

Il Est Né

Il est né le di-vin En - fant, Jou-ez hautbois, ré-son-nez, mu - set - tes, Il est né le di-vin En - fant, Chan-tons tous son a - vè - ne - ment! Nous voi - ci dans cet heu - reux temps, An - non - cé par tous les pro - phè - tes Nous voi- ci dans cet heu - reux temps, Ap - pe - lé de nos voeux ar - dents!

Learning French by Singing French

Shortly after the Louisiana State-Adoption of our first book of French folk songs (1974), the authors did a series of demonstrations, the purpose being to show why and how singing French aids in learning to speak French. While working with a number of groups, teachers and children, we developed some basic, guiding concepts and an overall procedure. That which follows is a brief presentation thereof, and is presented herewith in the hope that it may be helpful to teachers of French, music and classroom teachers.

A. Why Sing French?

Sung French aids in learning spoken French. In both, music and spoken French, the ear is involved. Music is an aural experience; spoken French is also. They effectively supplement each other. "There is no better aid to the learning of spoken French than singing French." This statement, in essence, was made by two outstanding leaders in the Louisiana Bilingual Program, one a widely respected administrator, and the other a talented, effective young teacher from France.

Such a broad premise as the above needs to be supported by specifics.

1. <u>Intoning</u>   Singing is the <u>intoning</u> of words or syllables (parts of words). This intoning - adding the element of pitch - aids in the <u>articulation</u> and <u>pronunciation</u> of given language sounds. Further, it helps to give <u>flow</u> to such sounds, thus promoting the concept and process of conversational flow.

2. <u>Rhythm</u>   A basic element of singing, <u>rhythm</u> yields surprising results in the learning of <u>verbal</u> <u>patterns</u>. The words of a song are, of course, verbal patterns.

3. <u>Repetition</u>   Songs, especially folk songs, often involve <u>repetition</u>, a must factor in language learning. Children (and adults) tend to enjoy repetition in songs; often they do not in verbal (spoken) exercises.

4. <u>Retention</u>   Melody, rhythm and repetition (in songs) tend to reinforce <u>retention</u> - of sounds, words, phrases, ideas.

5. <u>Enjoyment</u>   Singing, especially in view of the variety and change of pace factors, brings <u>enjoyment</u> to the language learning experience.

B. Procedure

The steps set forth below for teaching French folk songs in a bilingual program were, naturally, drawn from the foregoing list of specifics, especially rhythm, melody and repetition. It will be noted that we have chosen a "this is how we did it" manner of presenting these steps because these activities and this order worked best for us. However, such does not preclude flexibility to meet varying circumstances.

As to the song types. Especially at the outset, it is important to be mindful of the type of song chosen. Look for these characteristics: a marked rhythm; even, balanced phrases; repetition, in melody, rhythm and words; if possible, an obvious rhyme scheme; an attractive idea in the lyrics. Examples of such songs are: Il a Tout Dit, A Paris, Ton Thé?, Mon Bon Vieux Mari, Elle Descend de la Montagne, Ah! Mon Beau Chateau, Devinez, Bon Jour Mes Amis, Qu'il Fait Chaud, Sur le Plancher, Y a un Rat, D'Où Viens-Tu Bergère and Vive le Vent. (More)

Learning French by Singing French
(Continued)

1. The words, spoken and tapped in rhythm, came first. In the early stages, and
    especially with children of the mid elementary grades, the words were written
    in large letters on posterboard, ranging in size from 28 X 22 inches to 38 X 28.
    Markers of varied colors were used for lettering. Short songs or phrases were
    used at the start. Words of more than one syllable were hyphenated, and ordered
    on the posterboard so that phrases (or lines) would line-up, and repetitions
    could be pointed out. The "poster-song" was placed in the front of the class.
    The teacher spoke the words, in rhythm, pointing while speaking, slowly and
    rhythmically. (Use a dowel rod for a pointer.) Individuals were asked to
    point and speak, in rhythm. Then, all were asked to tap the rhythm of the
    words (tap fingers of one hand on the back of the other hand) as they spoke -
    with the teacher, and with leaders called up by her. (About the posterboard:
    the idea, of course, is to center attention, for pointing, speaking, tapping,
    singing, in the initial stage, before going to individual use of song books
    on the student's desk.)

2. Next, children were asked to listen to the melody as it was played or sung,
    while looking at and tapping the rhythm of the words quietly. (We used a set
    of classroom songbells for playing the melody, and played and sang short
    lines or phrases, one after the other.)

3. The children, following the teacher (or a student leader) were invited to
    sing, short lines/phrases, one after the other. (Following a singing leader
    is best, a played melody, next best, and a taped rendition least good but
    can be made to work.) While the music notation could not be seen at this
    word-poster stage, repetitions in melody and rhythm were pointed out. Later,
    when books with words and the music notation were used, the pointing out
    of repetitions - words, melody, rhythm figures - could be even more graphi-
    cally demonstrated. And this was found to be important: The use of the repe-
    tition factor always had great carryover value in this visual/aural experience,
    namely, using sung French to aid spoken French.

4. Lastly, the children were asked to speak the words again (as they were pointed
    to, and not necessarily in rhythm) so that the teacher (and children) could
    judge the degree to which the singing (intoning) had aided the speaking.
    Naturally, songs thus learned made possible a classroom repertoire for singing
    in French. About translation - giving the children the meaning of that which
    they were singing: We did it, bit by bit, from the start, and at the end,
    being sure they understood what they were singing.

C. Materials/Teachers

Posterboard, colored markers, chalkboard, French song books, classroom songbells
or piano, autoharp and/or guitar.

Highly recommended: That bilingual/bicultural teachers enlist the collaboration of
a music teacher, and vice versa. Teach French through music, music through French.

Coda

There is a consensus to the effect that a bilingual/bicultural program should
have as a principal aim, that of transmitting the essence of a given culture,
and further, that folk songs fulfill this aim in an unsurpassed manner.

BIBLIOGRAPHY

(This is a cumulative bibliography in that, since 1970, it has been added to for successive endeavors. Such includes our Chantez, La Louisiane!, articles and lecture-demonstrations, and finally, Chantez Encore. An asterisk indicates source material used in this book.)

Adam, Gaston Eugène. *Chansons Françaises en Louisiane. Masters' thesis, Louisiana State University, Baton Rouge, La., 1950.

Blanchet, Catherine Brookshire. *Louisiana French Folk Song among Children in Vermilion Parish, 1942 - 54. Masters' thesis, University of Southwestern Louisiana, Lafayette, La., 1970.

Bos, A. Note sur le Créole que' l'On Parle à L'Ile Maurice, Ancienne Ile de France. Romania, IX, 1880.

Bradley, Ruth. *Chants et Jeux. Lafayette, La., Lafayette Parish Schools, 1972.

Brandon, Elizabeth. *The Socio-Cultural Traits of the French Folksong in Louisiana. Revue de Louisiane, v. 1, no. 2, Lafayette, La., CODOFIL, 1972.

Broussard, James F. Louisiana Creole Dialect. Port Washington, N. Y., Kennikat Press, 1972.

Cable, George Washington. *Creole Slave Songs. Century Magazine, April 1886.

. The Dance in the Place Congo. Century Magazine, February 1886.

Courlander, Harold. Haiti Singing. Chapel Hill, University of North Carolina Press, 1939.

. Negro Folk Music, U.S.A. New York, Columbia University Press, 1963.

Fortier, Alcée. The French Language in Louisiana and the Negro-French Dialect. Transactions of the Modern Language Association of America, I, 1884-85.

Gudin, Jacqueline. Voici des Rondes. Paris, Editions Fleurus, 31 rue de Fleurus, 1976.

Gilmore, Jeanne L., and Robert C. *Chantez, La Louisiane! Lafayette, La., Acadiana Music, 1970.

Harrison, J. A. The Creole Patois of Louisiana. American Journal of Philology, III, 1882.

Hearn, Lafcadio. Two Years in the French West Indies, v. 3-4, Martinique Sketches. Boston, Houghton Mifflin, 1922.

Jameson, R. P., et A. E. Heacox. Chants de France. Boston, D.C. Heath, 1922.

*Jeunesse Qui Chante. (350 Chansons Anciennes) Paris, Les Editions Ouvrières, 12, Avenue Soeur-Rosalie, 1976.

(More)

Krehbiel, Henry Edward. _Afro-American Songs, a Study in Racial and National Music_. New York, G. Schirmer, 1914.

Landeck, Beatrice. _Echoes of Africa in the Folk Songs of the Americas_. New York, David McKay, 1961.

LeJeune, Emilie. _Creole Folk Songs_. Louisiana Historical Quarterly, v. II, 1919.

Our Acadian Heritage. Baton Rouge, Louisiana State Department of Education, 1955.

Monroe, Mina. *_Bayou Ballads, Twelve Folk-Songs from Louisiana_. (Creole) New York, G. Schirmer, 1921.

Oster, Harry. *_Folksongs of the Louisiana Acadians_. (Recording with notes) Arhoolie Records, 1959.

Morand, Simone. *_Anthologie de la Chanson de Haute Bretagne_. Paris, G. P. Maisonneuve et Larose, 11, rue Victor-Cousin, 1976.

Read, William A. _Creole and "Cajun"_. American Speech, v. I, 1925-26.

Sachs, Curt. _Rhythm and Tempo_. New York, W. W. Norton, 1953.

Scarborough, Dorothy. _On the Trail of Negro Folk-Songs_. Cambridge, Mass., Harvard University Press, 1925.

Theriot, Marie del Norte, and Catherine Brookshire Blanchet. *_Les Danses Rondes, Louisiana French Folk Dances_. Abbeville, La., 1955.

Thomson, Virgil. *_Acadian Songs and Dances_ from "Louisiana Story" (score and recording). New York, G. Schirmer, 1951. (Decca record, DL 9616)

Tinker, Edward Larocque. _Louisiana Gombo_. Yale Review, n.s., XXI, 1932.

Wehrmann, Henri. *_Creole Songs of the Deep South_. New Orleans, Philip Werlein, 1946.

Whitfield, Irène Thérèse. *_Louisiana French Folk Songs_. New York, Dover Publications, 1969.

ALPHABETICAL LIST OF SONGS